ISSN 0313.657X

OCCASIONAL PAPER NO.6

HUNTING AND GATHERING: THE FORAGE ECONOMY OF THE SIWAI OF BOUGAINVILLE

JOHN CONNELL

John Connell is a graduate of University College, London, and the University of Sussex. As a geographer with leanings towards economics and anthropology, his main concern in research has been with labour utilization and migration. He has worked in the U.K., in Africa and in Iran, and published extensively. In 1974 he was appointed a Research Associate with the Council for Pacific Development Studies and a Visiting Fellow with the Department of Economics, Research School of Pacific Studies, Australian National University.

National Library of Australia
Cataloguing-in-publication entry

Connell, John.
Hunting and gathering.

(Occasional paper; no.6)
ISBN 0 909150 24 9

1. Siuai (Papuan people). 2. Hunting, Primitive - Bougainville Island. I.Title. (Series: Australian National University, Canberra. Development Studies Centre. Occasional paper; no.6)

301.29935

ISSN 0313-637X

Printed and manufactured in Australia
by The Australian National University,
Canberra.

Distributed by the Development Studies Centre,
The Australian National University, Canberra.

Summary

This is the first account of a Bougainvillian society's hunting and gathering activities. The Siwai are a gardening people, and the greater part of their food requirements comes from the gardens, supplemented by trade store purchases. But hunting and gathering are traditional and are carried on partly for the pleasure derived from the activities, partly to make interesting additions to the diet. As the foraging is selective, there is no sign of a serious depletion of flora or fauna.

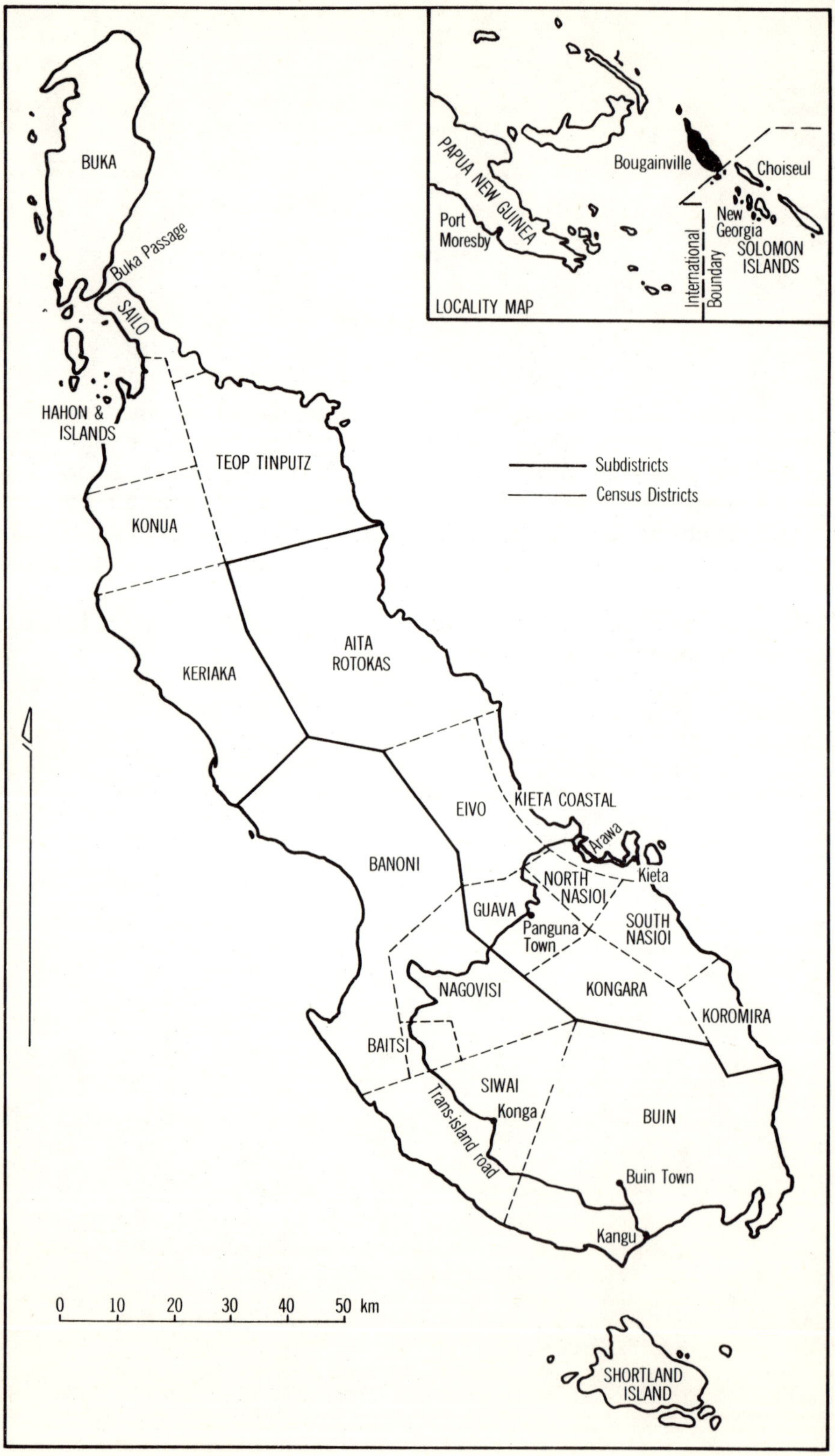

Bougainville

Foreword

Data for this paper were collected during a seventeen-month period (between October 1974 and April 1976) in the two Siwai villages of Maisua and Siroi. Siwai is a matrilineal society in South Bougainville, Papua New Guinea, with a population of around 9000 in 1975. Siwai culture was previously studied by Douglas L. Oliver in 1938-39 and is the subject of his book *A Solomon Island Society*, when the area and its people were then referred to as Siuai. Now there is unanimous agreement on the alternative spelling. I have indicated Siwai words by initially marking them with 'S'.

Acknowledgements

I am indebted to E.K. Fisk, D. Laycock, D.L. Oliver and A.H. Voyce for their comments on an earlier version of this paper.

Note: Prior to 1966 PNG currency was in pounds and shillings (designated £ and s.). After this it became dollars and cents ($ and c.). In 1975 PNG adopted its own currency which is kinas and toeas (K and t.) but these terms are not used in this paper.

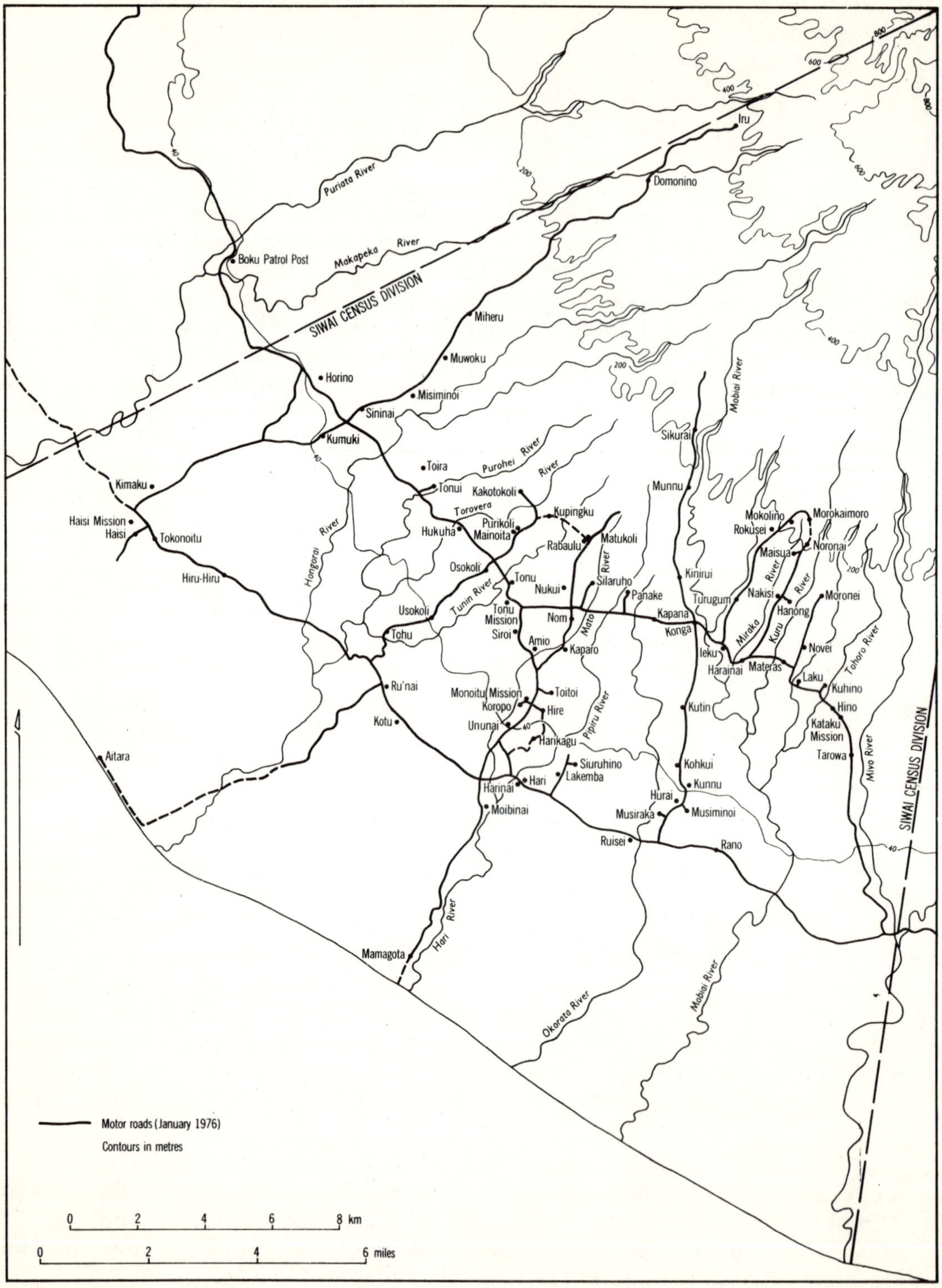

Motor roads (January 1976)
Contours in metres
0 2 4 6 8 km
0 2 4 6 miles
SIWAI CENSUS DIVISION
Boku Patrol Post
Kumuki
Tonu Mission
Monoitu Mission
Haisi Mission
Kataku Mission

Siwai

Hunting and Gathering: The Forage Economy of the Siwai of Bougainville

> The superior knowledge which these natives possess of each plant and its uses has often led me to reflect on the meagre acquaintance with the commonest trees, shrubs and herbs which the ordinary white man can claim.
>
> (H.B. Guppy, The Solomon Islands and their Natives, London 1887, p.280)

The Siwai have a single story of the very remote past when they were simply a gathering people, their only food being collected from a range of readily available trees and bushes. After *Tantanu* (Maker) showed them how to plant food crops, gardening replaced collecting and a gardening economy became established, surviving unchanged for a very long time. There are no stories concerning the origin of hunting (pigs, possums or other animals and birds) nor are there stories of fishing (either in the sea or rivers); each of these parts of the economy has also been in existence a very long time and probably date at least from the same time as the mythical origin of agriculture. Indeed one of the Siwai spiritual beings *(S-kupunas)*, Panana (Orphan), invented improved hunting and fishing techniques (Oliver 1955:43). The long historical continuity in the different forms of obtaining wild food is reflected in a general absence of perceived changes, except in the technology of hunting. The range and quantity of foods that can be collected seem to have changed little and to be changing only slowly, even in the more densely populated central Siwai area. This may not necessarily be true; an absolute decline in quantity would easily be offset by a change in food preferences on the part of some Siwais. The low population density in south Bougainville ensures a large area of bush, in some areas almost virgin rainforest, in other areas undisturbed for one or more decades. This bush provides a wide range of edible plant species and a habitat for a number of kinds of hunted game. Indeed the range of available resources is very great despite the depletion in fauna and flora eastwards through Melanesia. This paper considers the nature of these resources and the use that Siwais make of wild or presently uncultivated[1] planted species.

Hunting

Siwais believe that there has been a decline in the availability of game of every kind; so great has it been that the Local Government Council has attempted to legislate against some kinds of hunting. Perhaps symbolic of this decline is the almost total absence of both the eagle *(S-monko)* and the

---

[1]Formerly wild species such as bananas, betel palms, breadfruit and some kinds of nuts are not considered here since there are now few wild species of these trees that provide fruit.

hornbill *(S-huhu)*, the totems of the two major moieties within Siwai; in seventeen months I saw only four hornbills and one eagle, and this eagle had already been captured. Hornbills are a little more common in more mountainous areas of Bougainville but the eagle, a coastal bird, has almost disappeared from the island. The taboos that prevent members of a clan eating their own totem have not ensured these birds' survival. Paradoxically they seem to be the only two species whose demise is imminent. The number of wild pigs and possums, the main hunted species, has also fallen considerably but possibly only since the war.

Oliver's descriptions of hunting before the war imply that there already seemed to have been a decline in pig hunting: 'the wild pig hunts of former days required scores of men' (Oliver 1955: 311). Which declined first, the spirit of co-operation or the number of pigs, is unknown and the story may reflect no more than a familiar vision of a bountiful past. As early as 1930 in the most densely populated part of Bougainville, the Nasioi were already stating that possums,birds and fish had been much more plentiful in the past (Blackwood 1931:427). Game has always been declining but there is no suggestion that possum hunting was similarly declining. Population growth in historic times must have been very slow and the consequences of a change from a stone to steel economy, either in increased areas of cultivation or in more efficient spears, is unlikely to have made significant inroads into the numbers of wild fauna. It seems probable that the steady population increase of the twentieth century was only just beginning to reduce the numbers of huntable species significantly when the war intervened.

The most significant change in Siwai hunting was the introduction of the gun. Although the Siwai Local Government Council had a gun in 1961, this was solely to meet requests to the Council to shoot birds eating rice and corn in Siwai gardens. The Council policeman was the marksman; the hire was set at 1s for simply scaring away birds and 2s if the bird was killed and eaten. Guns were not generally available until later in the 1960s; in 1975 they cost around $40 to $45 but sales ended in the same year. Most villages now have one or two shotguns. By 1969 there was growing concern over the disappearance of game and control was sought by limiting the area that an individual could hunt in to the land of his own matrilineage only. Thus the Morokaimoro people recommended that anyone who caught game in another's land would pay $2 for each animal taken and the Council discussed imposing a total ban on hunting access to other lineage's ground. In 1973 an agenda item was raised to prevent more Siwais buying guns; it was not passed. The Miheru councillor complained that there were not yet any guns in his area whilst the Kumuki councillor thought that a ban should refer only to central Siwai. In 1975 the Council tried again; as one councillor pointed out, 'soon children will not know what a possum is'. The Mamagota councillor recommended that only men who owned ground should be allowed shotguns (but backed down in agreeing that guns had a secondary use for shooting flying foxes in cocoa plantations). A separate move attempted to restrict bows and arrows but the councillors agreed with Korike of Mamagota who pointed out that 'people with bows and arrows don't feel that they have to return with something'. As usual no motion was passed; the Council ended soon afterwards and village governments concerned themselves with political problems. Purchase of guns ended but sales of cartridges and reduction of game continued unabated.

Pigs

Hunting of wild pigs *(S-huru)* was beginning to decline before the war but there were obvious regional variations; 'in southern Siwai natives may go for a year or more without eating wild pig and during my fifteen week residence in one northern village (Turugum) only two wild pigs were killed' (Oliver 1955:30), whilst in Morokaimoro, which is on the fringe of the rain forest, pork from this source is more frequently forthcoming' (Oliver 1949 (3):7).

Attitudes to hunting varied; indeed Oliver stated both that 'hunting pigs is more of a sport than a serious economic enterprise' (ibid.) and 'hunting for wild pigs is in fact a serious undertaking requiring skill, persistence and some courage' (1955:30). Wild pig meat is neither essential to nutrition nor to feast requirements. Moreover Oliver records one informant's statement that *'Potu* (prestige) cannot be speared in the forest' (1949 (3):7), whilst domesticated European-type pigs were such an improvement in size and succulence over the typically thin wild pigs that this difference alone was considered by Siwais to be enough to discourage hunting (ibid.:8).

Historically, pig hunts were grand affairs. 'Until recent years wild-pig drives involved up to a hundred men. A stockade was constructed, then the hunters would unleash their dogs, form a wide circle and converge on the stockade ... shouting and blowing on conch shells. Pigs driven into the stockade were then speared. Very large scale and successful drives are said to have netted up to thirty pigs ... now and then a hunter or a dog would be maimed or even killed' (Oliver 1955:30-1). The combination of skill and courage in obtaining food is familiar. Although there may still have been pig-hunting teams before the war (Oliver 1949 (4):58) it seems to have been primarily an activity restricted to a few individuals. 'The customary hunting method is for one man to start off with dogs and roam through the forest until the dogs find and run down an animal which is then killed by a long throwing spear made of hard limbum palm' (Oliver 1955:30). Pig traps may also have existed (Oliver 1949 (1):9).

The returns from pig hunting were not great. In 1939 Kummai of Morokaimoro was the most famous hunter in northeast Siwai; he spent about a fifth of his time at it and managed to bring in one or two pigs a month (Oliver 1949 (3):7). But most hunting was much less systematic; Ho'oma of Turugum saw signs of a wild pig's depredations in his garden, returned home for his dogs and spears and captured the pig within a couple of hours (ibid.). On another occasion, however, Ho'oma went off towards the Mivo River, where game could have been expected to be more plentiful, and returned after three days with only a single wild pig (Oliver 1955:432). This was a more usual expenditure of time than when on rare occasions a wild pig ventured close to a garden. Usually the pig was eaten by the hunter's family; in some cases it was cooked in the men's club house, and eaten by the men only. In either case it was not as good as domesticated pig.

Wild pig hunting seems to have declined little since before the war but is now increasingly confined to the margins of Siwai settlement, especially to the north and south where the bush is densest and least disturbed. How many pigs remain is, of course, quite impossible to estimate but in mid-1956 there were reported to be enough wild pigs for the old practice of allowing them to service domestic sows to have returned (Hook 1956). In central Siwai wild pigs are usually absent although one was killed near Tonu in 1975, but pig hunters must go to the fringes of Siwai. Occasionally wild pigs still damage gardens but escaped domestic pigs are a more usual hazard. Pig hunting was invariably an individual affair for a specialist and his dogs, although sometimes these dogs might be hired by a group of friends. The organization of hunting remained unchanged; dogs would eventually corner the pig, which would be either speared or, preferably, if a group of men were present, captured alive and carried back to the village. It was claimed that the Japanese had demonstrated an improved kind of pig trap that caught pigs by their legs rather than their heads but pig trapping was unusual and generally unsuccessful, although the leading hunters would maintain regular traps nearer their villages.

In the central Siwai area the leading hunter was Tubana, a Kotu man in his fifties, who hunted with his four dogs in the bush between his home and the beach. He managed to catch pigs at the rate of about one every two months, with perhaps a day's effort in each case. At other times Tubana hired out his dogs at $2 per day. Sometimes hunting was contract work; in October 1975 some Siroi villagers wanted a pig for a party and paid him $5 for a day's work. The resulting pig was comparable with a domestic pig that would have been sold for about $50. On other occasions Tubana would distribute pieces to his own kin and on one occasion pieces were sold at a party that he had organized. The total value of these pieces was about $30. Even more occasionally pig pieces may be sold for similar prices at one of the Siwai markets.

In contrast to the prewar period wild pig meat was invariably preferred to domestic pig; it was strong and had no fat. But for most purposes wild pigs are inferior. It would be an insult to offer a wild pig at a mortuary feast or on any other ceremonial occasion. It is exactly the same in Buin. Laycock (pers. comm. 1976) observed a Buin man attempting to provide a wild pig at a party in place of the domestic pig that had been ordered; he was rightly told that this form of cheating would not be tolerated. Parties are not ceremonials; at my own farewell party Maisua villagers caught a wild pig that was a welcome addition to the domestic pigs. Consequently wild pig pieces are bought and sold for domestic consumption, which would be unheard of for domestic pig meat; hunting is, in a sense, a 'cheap' way of providing pork. In twelve months Siroi villagers caught one wild pig and in five months Maisua also caught one. This suggests that throughout Siwai around fifty pigs were the approximate total bag of a year's hunting - a product of about three times as many hunting trips. Pig hunting, where a shotgun is of no particular assistance, is not at present declining.

Possums

Possum hunting seems to have remained almost unchanged in the prewar years; no technological changes influenced the style of hunting, there were no domesticated substitutes and no apparent depletion in numbers. There may even have been some movement from pig to possum hunting. Possum hunting was no more than an 'adventurous outing' (Oliver 1955:31) since the risks (tree climbing) were well known and not as unpredictable as those of pig hunting. Unlike wild pigs, possums *(S-napa)* were essential for almost all feasts and ceremonies, for some of which they had to be alive. Indeed their ritual and symbolic significance seems remarkably similar to that in areas as far west as Seram (Ellen 1972).

Possum hunting had also remained a group activity. Some villages such as Turugum had well organized teams which functioned frequently (Oliver 1955:311-2), but usually two or three boys or men would be enough. A possum would be 'treed, sometimes with the help of dogs [and] a younger native will climb the tree and shake down the possum while his companions wait on the ground to pounce on the stunned animal' (Oliver 1955:31). Occasionally traps were set over an 'oppossum trail'; these were 'ingenious but rarely successful' (ibid.). The productivity of possum hunting seems to have been rather greater than wild pig hunting. Oliver notes that 'one hunting expedition ... spent two days and nights in the forest north of Mokorino village. It covered, roughly, a three square mile area, drained it of animals, they said, and brought back a bag of 48 opposums' (Oliver 1955: 481). The size of the party is unstated.

Possum hunting has been changed significantly in the last decade by the introduction of guns. The traditional method of finding the animals remains the same: dogs sniff out likely trees but there is now no need to climb. Given the general dislike for tree climbing (Oliver 1955:31) and the considerable difficulty involved in climbing sago trees, the usual haunt of possums, present strategies are a vast improvement in efficiency. The possums are blinded and transfixed with a strong torch whilst they can be shot and dogs are ready to pounce on slightly wounded possuns. However, possums that are intended for some kinds of ritual use primarily 'washing', must be captured alive so that they are alive during the ceremony and can subsequently be ritually killed. Almost invariably possum hunting takes place at night since possums are nocturnal animals; a hunting party usually consists of no more than three or four men, since a larger group could not move quietly, and this may break up into individuals or pairs during the hunting. Usually such an expedition lasts for three or four hours, ending around midnight. Occasionally demands are such that more desperate tactics are employed. On one occasion I accompanied a daytime hunting party of four youths and two dogs which found a succession of likely sago trees; each was chopped down until a possum finally fell out of the fourth and was seized. The expedition was over. There is little concern for immature sago trees and none for immature possums; mothers with babies are just as desirable.

Possums remain essential for feasts and ceremonies and with a recent increase in the number of ceremonies demand too has increased and there is a general concern about the decline in possum numbers. Nevertheless it is not difficult to find possums, even in the most densely populated parts of Siwai, and they are rarely far away from villages. (Several individuals, who had moved away from the village lines to individual houses dispersed in the bush, told me that one of the reasons for this and one of the rewards was the much better returns to hunting. In the peace of the bush they were able to hear animals at night rather than go out looking for them.)

For a fortunate hunter, with a gun, returns can be very high. Uming, a young man from Amio, caught fifteen possums in a couple of nights in the Ru'nai area, but on the third night a spirit *(S-mara)*, which he was certain was that of a Siwai killed during the war by the Japanese, followed him round. He caught no possums and gave up before midnight. (This was his contribution to a feast following the death of his father. For his own purposes, despite the saleability of possums, he would have been unlikely to spend more than one night catching two or three of them.) At the same time a group of four men from Kaparo spent the whole night hunting in their own area, finding only one old possum, without a tail and with one eye missing; the bag was disappointing and the ancient possum was the omen of another imminent death. An individual going into the bush at night for a few hours of possum hunting was more than likely to be successful; nevertheless in a central village like Siroi, where there was only one shotgun, no more than one possum a fortnight would be brought back to the village. The success rate was never high enough to tempt many night-time hunters; the distant bush is no place to be at night and almost all nocturnal expeditions were by small groups.

Other Hunting Activities

The main hunting activities before the war were those involving pigs and possums; other species seem to have been relatively unimportant quarries. Then Siwais used to

> capture and eat tree-rats and eels but reject house rats, snakes and lizards. Now and then they shoot or net flying foxes and some kinds of birds, but make little effort to exploit the forests' many other resources in edible flying things. The occasionally eat grubs and certain kinds of spiders and ants (Oliver 1955:12).

Nevertheless few Siwais had actually caught or even eaten tree rats, but soups made from flying foxes and flying mice were a favourite though infrequent food (Oliver 1955:31). Flying foxes and mice were shot with specially designed pronged arrows, and birds with ordinary arrows (Oliver 1949 (1):9). It seems that all of these small animals have historically played a small role in hunting and consequently in diet supplementation; none seems to have been the object of special forays into the bush.

If guns have generally improved the returns to possum hunting, they have almost totally changed the hunting of high-flying birds and mammals. Oliver makes no mention of prewar eagle and hornbill hunting; now these have almost disappeared. The several species of flying foxes are eagerly sought after, although they are bony and their meat is strong and not as well liked as that of possums. Although a sporadic dusk activity in many villages is firing of bows and arrows at the rapidly swooping flying foxes, hitting one, even when they feed in the almond and breadfruit trees, is almost impossible. Guns are more successful, even if most hunters regard the one or two cartridges required (at 20c each) as too expensive to justify the effort. This and the low taste preference make flying foxes an irregular component of the diet.

Several species of birds, but especially white pigeons, are favourite targets for hunters but they are not particularly common and are fast moving and difficult to shoot. Certain areas known to be a haunt of pigeons are visited regularly by hunters, one Osokoli man visiting relatives at Lamuai on the Buin coast, borrowed an outboard motor and visited a small island off the coast. In an hour he had a bag of four pigeons; in Siwai that sort of return would usually be impossible. Pigeons, like pigs and possums, are now something for which it is worth mounting a special expedition. Guns have made that possible.

Inevitably many hunting expeditions come back with mixed bags especially when the object is to provide a boost to the meat requirements of a feast. One group of five Siroi men returned from five hours of night hunting with three possums, three pigeons, two flying foxes, a tree rat, a frog and a lizard, all obtained within a mile of the village; they complained that had more men gone their bag would have been much greater. On another occasion six hours' hunting produced no more than one flying fox, but the likely bag from a night's activity is almost always closer to that of the first example. There is no shortage of the smaller animals that simply do not justify special efforts to find them whilst some, like tree rats *(S-kamari)*, are very difficult to catch and others, like frogs, are

Plate 1. The result of a night's hunting near Siroi; birds and possums, a flying fox, a lizard and a frog.

Plate 2. Possum caught near Siroi troughs.

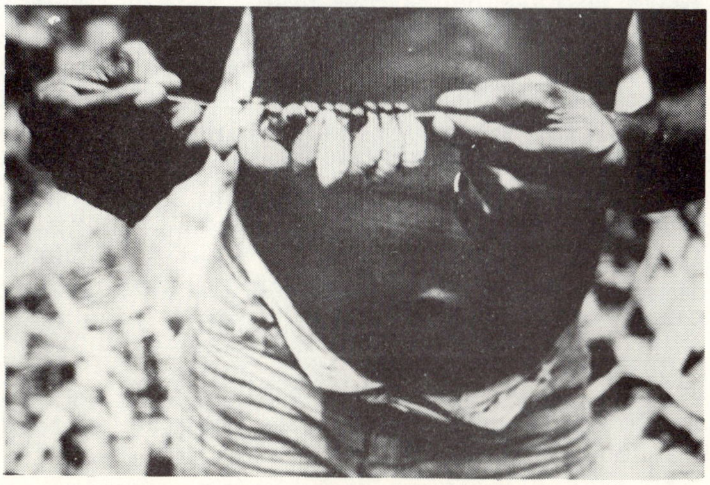

Plate 3. Sago grubs collected in Turugum

not ubiquitously welcome in the average Siwai diet.

Guns make hunting easier but there is a much greater triumph in catching game with a bow and arrow and few households do not have them Moreover bows and arrows have a flexibility in use that the licensed gun can never achieve. On one occasion I saw a Siwai spot a cockatoo in a nearby tree; unhurriedly he finished shaping a limbum palm stick, twisted some vines into a draw string, cut some sago leaf ribs for arrows and in less than half an hour he was able to shoot at the bird, and miss.

Fishing

On the east coast of Bougainville, sheltered by reefs, sea fishing has always provided a steady supply of food to coast dwellers but on the Siwai coast high surf makes fishing dangerous and not very productive. On the east coast inland dwellers received fish from the coastal people in exchanges; in Siwai they usually went without. Oliver observed that inland Siwais travelled to the coast to collect shells but did 'not trouble with fishing while there' (Oliver 1955:12). Coastal Siwais almost certainly did some fishing in the prewar period. River fishing was more frequent but did not add significantly to Siwai diets. Men often wandered individually along the course of a stream searching for fish and eels to be caught with bow and arrow, 'hopeful but rarely successful' (Oliver 1955:31). In addition to these individual and spasmodic attempts, villages sometimes also engaged in co-operative fish drives which, beside the larger rivers, might occur as often as two or three times a year. The main technique was to divert water from a stream by damming it and shoot or capture the fish and prawns left floundering in the pools. In one such effort about eighty Siwais took part and caught about 200 pounds of fish and several hundred prawns (ibid.). Group hunting and fishing activities were the only examples of co-operation for economic motives beyond the household or hamlet.

Sea fishing has grown since the war; several Aitara and Mamagota villagers have purchased nets and fish irregularly from canoes. Some Haisi and Ruisei villagers also own canoes.[2] Production at present is small; although none of the Siwai markets was ever supplied with fresh or smoked fish from the Siwai coast some Aitara villagers regularly sold fish when they left the village or when other Siwais visited Aitara.

There seems always to have been some fish trade between the coast and inland villages; in 1950 Franke observed a 'very slight' trade with fish as long as wrist to elbow worth 3s and from fingertip to elbow 4s (Franke 1950). Fish sizes are designated in the same way as the girth of pigs. In 1975 Aitara villagers were selling smoked fish weighing between 5 and 10 pounds for $7 to $10 each to inland Siwais. But isolated Aitara is exceptional; no Aitara villager yet owns any significant amount of cocoa, hence incomes are much lower than in the rest of Siwai. I have no good data on the amount of cash earned by Aitara villagers from fishing but based on estimates of coastal-inland trade several villagers certainly earned over $100 in the year

---

[2] Different matrilineages claim ownership of different sections of the sea. (I am not clear how far out this ownership is considered to extend, probably as far as two tiny islands about a mile from the coast.) In theory individuals from different clans must apply for permission to fish on the coast and could be expected to pay a small levy; in practice this does not happen so there is no constraint upon fishing by inland Siwais. (Access to the beach at Mamagota was controlled by one clan head there who was concerned less with fishing than with the morals of Siwai youth!)

from fish sales. Elsewhere no Siwais sold sea fish in 1975 and probably never have done. Sporadically attempts have been made to commercialize production; nets and outboard motors were given to Aitara villagers in 1972 and a three-day school was organized there, but almost inevitably distance prevented development. When a Siwai instructor at Buin Vocational School tried to interest Haisi villagers in commercial production in 1974 the original glimmer of interest had disappeared into cocoa. The small quantities of salt-water fish that are consumed in Siwai come mainly from the Shortland Islands. Indeed Siwais are primarily 'bush people' rather than 'salt-water people', and have remarkably little interest in coastal resources.

Even more exceptional salt-water delicacies are sea turtles which migrate to the Siwai coast for a limited period of the year. Inland, techniques of capture and killing are unknown; when Siroi villagers purchased a turtle for $10 in 1975 a Mamagota villager came along to do the killing and cutting up of the animal. Turtle meat is much prized but it is a rare delicacy, usually only incorporated into occasional feasts. Dugongs were once caught in coastal waters but the whales that occasionally passed through the Bougainville Strait never seem to have come aground on the Siwai coast.

Rarest of all are crocodiles; the scars on some older men clearly indicate that hunting (and avoiding) crocodiles was much more common in the past. They still exist in the coastal swamps at least between Aitara and the Mivo and are always a source of fear to the wary Siwai, but it is several years since they were systematically hunted and shot since numbers declined with the arrival some time after the war of European hunters. In 1965 a *kiap* (patrol officer) recommended that 'encouragement should be given to local shooters instead of the European professionals who are rapidly thinning out the numbers of crocodiles in the numerous Empress Augusta Bay rivers' (Reading 1965). Until around 1966 a European trader ran a shipping service along the west coast, purchasing copra and crocodile skins, and doing some shooting himself. In 1969 Pasua of Kunnu and some Aitara villagers complained to the *kiap* about unlicensed crocodile shooters who spent four weeks between Tonolei and Torokina, shooting at least one crocodile near Aitara (French 1969). Pasua was then the only Siwai with a licence; since then he has not bothered to hunt them although he was fond of remarking that he would soon start again. The crocodile skins were sold and some of the meat, especially that of the tail, eaten.

Like the sea, rivers in Siwai are owned so that access is restricted by lineage membership. In effect this tends to ensure that the large, productive rivers, especially the Hongorai and Mivo, are not overfished since I recorded no instances of these being rented out. In the 1960s illegal dynamiting was beginning to deplete these rivers but court action reversed this trend. Fishing by individual males with nets and lines is the usual procedure in the larger rivers where fish larger than 10 pounds can sometimes be found. (I was unfamiliar with villages close to these rivers; although some villagers did sell substantial numbers of freshwater fish, the majority were certainly eaten within the fisherman's household). Occasionally fish may be poisoned with the leaves of *Derris* spp. *(S-tung)*. Like hunting, fishing activity increases when a ceremonial places greater demands on meat supplies. At Christmas time, too, fish is a preferred food. Several inland Siwais make their single annual visit to the coast around Christmas to purchase, or even try their hand at catching fish. Times are changing slowly; in the early 1880s Guppy 'came upon some bushmen from the interior of Bougainville who, although they were staying some time at a village on the coast of Fauro (in the Bougainville Straits), would not eat fish' (Guppy 1887:91).

Bow and arrow fishing is totally absent in Siwai now and seems to have disappeared from almost all of Bougainville. In the small rivers and streams there is no systematic fishing activity of this kind but stone fish, gudgeons, perch and other small fish are caught by 'glassing'; men and youths wearing goggles dive amongst the stones spearing fish and occasionally eels. Grilled over a fire they eventually make no more than a tasty snack but, as an interlude on a hot day, it is an exceptionally pleasant and rewarding form of exercise. I saw only one fish trap in Siwai and as far as I know there were no communal fish drives in 1975. In the past the most popular river for fishing drives was the larger Hongorai; traps could be as large as 30 feet by 20 feet and engage a whole village or area in its construction (Voyce, pers. comm. 1976). There is nothing like this now; once again surplus energy is more usually channelled into cocoa growing and communal effort has given way to individual enterprise.

Gathering

Fauna

Shellfish, sago grubs and prawns are gathered rather than hunted; other creatures like the green grasshopper *(S-massa)*, are gathered if they stay still. Nothing would justify chasing them. Green leaf snails *(S-kaiyori)* are occasionally collected to be made into lime. Little has changed from before the war. Oliver notes: 'Collecting edible insects is only an incidental activity - if natives see them they may try to collect them ... the Siwai like to eat beetles, white ants and certain kinds of spiders' (1955:30). Voyce considered that Oliver was misled and that Siwai never ate white ants or beetles; although they occasionally ate red ants *(S-sumiko)* they would be humiliated if it was thought that they ate beetles (1957:107). I have never seen or heard of Siwais eating any of these and usually when I requested a massa it was claimed that these were rarely eaten nowadays. Leaf snails may sometimes be eaten. Other possibilities are rarer although there are always those who claim to have eaten dogs, rats and even wild domesticated cats.

For anyone, male or female, child or adult, no visit to the coast would be complete without some attempt, however spasmodic, to collect some of the shellfish *(S-k'rua)* that burrow a few inches into the sand below the breaking waves. They contain food and, more important, when the shells are roasted and crushed they provide lime, essential to betel chewing and a component of several kinds of medicine. (Some Siwais still use a pair of large mussel shells for shaving.) No inland Siwai would visit the coast simply to obtain shells especially since collecting is hard work; indeed the normal source is a gift or purchase from coastal Siwais who also occasionally sell lime in the Siwai markets. For coastal Siwais mussel shell collecting is women's work.

Before the war sago grubs *(S-pa'to)* were 'regarded as a delicacy' (Oliver 1955:30); nowadays they are not apparently so generally popular and several Siwais express considerable distaste at the thought of eating them. The grubs live in the fractured trunks of fallen, cleared or cut sago trees and can easily be collected by chipping away the rotten bark and wood and removing the wriggling grub. This is usually women's work, the nearest female equivalent to hunting. Fried or boiled the grubs are delicious and a regular constituent of some diets; they are also a good nutritional balance to the starchy, dry sago flour.

Before the war women and girls, once a fortnight or so, spent a few hours wading in a stream searching by hand for prawns hiding under ledges and rocks whilst almost everywhere prawn traps were left in the rivers; 'nearly every two or three hundred feet of a stream's course will harbour one, but these remain empty for weeks at a time, and word of a catch becomes a lively conversation topic in the neighbourhood' (Oliver 1955:31). I suspect that this substantially underestimates the number of prawns removed from Siwai streams. Collecting prawns remains women's work although construction of the six-foot long basket-traps, from which all the prawns are collected, is men's work. (Specialist trap *(S-kaang)* makers are rare now in Siwai; Dingong, an old Siroi man, was capable of producing one every couple of months which he usually sold for $2). In the northeast streams, fish and prawns were usually smaller hence collections remain less than in central Siwai, where prawns were regular and much-welcomed additions to the meal. No household would go for more than three or four weeks without eating prawns, although they might not want to advertise this fact to their neighbours. Traps were set at specific times, often at night, and never left for long periods in the streams; the usual optimum period was after heavy rain when the rivers would flood. Then groups of women would go together to leave their traps; a few hours later they would return rarely empty-handed. Voyce (pers. comm. 1976) states that it was common even in 1975, and especially for Ruhuaku, for women to net prawns and fish. Laycock (pers. comm. 1976) observed Buins catching prawns by flipping them out of streams with a grass knife *(sarip)*, a technique I have not seen in Siwai. Prawns are the most succulent item of local food and streams and their banks are the most productive micro-environments in Siwai.

Flora

Before the war Oliver simply notes that the Siwai collected *'hari* nuts and many kinds of edible leaves, nuts, ferns, mushrooms and fungi from the forest; (Oliver 1955:30). Clearly there was not much regional variation in Siwai or Bougainville, nor had there been any changes over time. Indeed Oliver notes that a more detailed account is that given for the islands of the Bougainville Strait in 1884 (Guppy 1887). In 1939 gathered foods constituted about 2 per cent of the weight of an ordinary meal (Oliver 1955: 30), although its nutritional component was much higher. Once again little has changed although the number of species consumed by many households has declined.

(a) Canarium almonds. Canarium almonds *(Canarium* spp., S-*moi)* are one of the most valuable naturally occurring tree crops in Siwai. However their produce, galip nuts, have historically been of much greater importance in Bougainville. Guppy observed how they were often stored in large quantities in the nineteenth century Solomons; he also noted how the Spanish discoverers of the Solomons under Mendaña seized and carried off to their ships great stores of them (1887:85). Ubiquitously they are a much loved food. Parkinson recorded that Bougainvilleans had designed a special stone mallet solely for the purpose of cracking the hard shells of the almonds (Parkinson 1907:438). Canarium almond trees grow throughout Bougainville and all parts of Siwai seem to be equally endowed with trees. Before the war Siwais regularly planted trees but possibly not so regularly in the northeast as in central Siwai. All of these were individually owned, although no tree would bear nuts until after around thirty years. There have been no new plantings of galips for some years and in good years nuts may even lie ignored on the ground; in 1934 the plant collector, J.H.L.Waterhouse, described Siwai as 'that remarkable country of big drums and dolmens and canarium cults and cremations; (Anon. 1934) but the 'cult' of the canarium has now almost disappeared.

Before the war the start of the galip season resulted in garden work being 'forsaken for a few days to allow time for collecting nuts and extracting the kernels ... picking is a hazardous undertaking ... Now and then someone will fall, and this occasionally proves fatal' (Oliver 1955: 28). (There are different kinds of canarium almonds in Siwai; those in the northeast being shorter are more easily climbed than those in the centre which even before the war were rarely climbed.) Several neighbourhoods had nutting teams which had a more or less fixed membership with both sexes and nearly all ages participating. Such a team would be rewarded by the tree owner with a special meal (Oliver 1955:311). Kernels were eaten whole and raw, mashed in a mortar and added to sago and taro puddings or smoked and stored for future use and trade. Some Rataiku hamlets actually specialized in smoking large quantities of nuts for sale or exchange; active feast givers had to arrange for supplies well in advance because of the shortness of the nut-ripening season, the large demand and the relatively limited supply (ibid.:298). At the height of the season sellers often sold out completely. Consequently 'the almond, more than any other Siwai economic plant, is purposefully harvested for sale' (ibid.:347); every Siwai village had two or three men who specialized in collecting and selling nuts. Oliver recorded that in one village four such specialists together sold almonds worth 350 fathoms of *mauai* in a season (ibid.:348).

The postwar decline in the use of almonds in feast-giving and trade has had several consequences, all stemming from the substantially reduced demand for the nuts. Nuts remain a minor component of feasting but are increasingly being replaced by rice and tinned fish although they are still important in 'washing' and growth magic ceremonies and are often a part of marriage transactions. There is no longer any formal long-distance trading; in two villages I found only one very old man, the widowed Kunke of Maisua, who systematically smoked and sold nuts as a significant source of income. Other villagers, usually children, collect nuts; most are immediately eaten raw but about a quarter are smoked to be stored for use in ordinary domestic meals or in pudding manufacture for feasts. Small quantities are made into puddings for sale in Siwai markets and equally small quantities are sold there as raw shelled nuts. No one receives much revenue from these sales but it represents a small income from nuts freely obtained. Smoked almonds are never sold in the markets although they are occasionally traded within Siwai; the price of one three-foot tube of smoked galips in 1975 was 50 cents. The usual Siwai explanation for the decline in interest in galip nuts was that cocoa sales provided a much better source of cash. Climbing of almond trees disappeared at much the same time that cocoa revenue entered Siwai in the mid-1960s.

Before the war the galip season ran from late July into October and apparently all the nuts were collected by climbing into the high trees. Now no Siwai ever climbs an almond tree, the most difficult of all to climb, and all nuts are collected from the ground, invariably by small children. No adult now collects nuts; Kunke received most of his galips from his grandchildren. Consequently the collecting season now extends into January and February.

Although all individual canarium almond trees have known owners, who usually trace ancestry from the planter rather than land owner, and the trees are inherited, usually patrilineally (Oliver 1955:344-5), this is no longer important. Their ownership is never discussed at *nori* payments where property inheritance may be challenged, and no Siwai would be prevented from collecting nuts from any tree in his own home area. In 1958 they were the most valuable tree crop worth £1 each (compared with 10s for sago and coconut palms) when compensation was awarded for their destruction at Konga but by 1966 at Tonu they were worth less, $1, compared with sago palms ($3) and coconuts ($2), but still worth $3 further east at Upakoli.[3] Their 'European' value was more or less static. Galips are now a free good and ownership is rarely enforced; any Siwai with time and patience can make a small income from collection and sale. Most prefer other sources of revenue.

Almost throughout the central Melanesian islands, at least from Bougainville to Malaita and even in the Indonesian island of Seram (Ellen 1975:139) the canarium almond (know as *ngali* in most parts of the Solomon Islands) seems to have had a similar historic importance, both economically and socially, although one that has almost disappeared except in the more remote upland areas. In the Baegu area of northern Malaita (Ross 1973:43), where the almond has a similar importance to that of pre-war Siwai, climbing (and even hiring of climbers) continues so that the season remains from August to October. Amongst the Eivo of central Bougainville the same is true and feasts are much more closely tied to the almond season there (M.P. Hamnett, pers. comm.) as also in Choiseul island (Scheffler 1965:4). Amongst the To'ambaita of northern Malaita work groups are organized to collect (by climbing the trees) and also to break the nuts, whilst almonds are important both in the coastal markets and local trade (Fraser, pers. comm. 1976). In Guava, the area now closest to Panguna copper mine, a traditional galip collecting system was still existing at least in 1955 to the extent that *kiaps* were advised not to conduct patrols between September and December, the harvest months, when people scattered into the bush.

> Each tree is owned. Men climb trees using ropes and hook down almonds. It is rumoured that it is so difficult to climb the tree that they stay there all day. Nuts are smoked and then sealed with leaves and wet ashes into bamboo tubes. They are then placed on house roofs where they can be kept for 3 or 4 years. Some tubes are sold for cash: others are kept for feasts at the end of the season - when wild pigs and possums are also caught (McCabe 1956).

In Solos, Buka (Sarei 1974:4) and in lowland Nasioi (Ogan 1972:37, 131), before the war the organization seems to have been similar to this but in neither area is galip collecting still socially important. In Buin galips were smoked and sold at least as recently as 1955 (Gow 1956) and in Banoni in 1956 (Hook 1957). In Buin the sale price was approximately 1s per pound and in Banoni 2s per section of bamboo (which was about 3 feet long and therefore probably about the same rate as in Buin). At Kurtatchi village, on the north coast of Bougainville, although almonds were collected only by women and girls, some were mixed with taro for ceremonial puddings but the nuts may not have been smoked or stored. The 'time of the almond' was an occasion for reciprocal feasts between villages and before 1930 there had also been a particular ceremony to mark the occasion of the ripening of the first almonds (Blackwood 1935:278-80). Nowhere is it explained why the almond was so important socially throughout these Melanesian islands but in several areas, as in Siwai, it is almost the only seasonal plant, hence year *(S-moi)* and almond are the same word. It is not improbable that ceremonials, often marking stages in life cycles, were timed to coincide with the fruiting of the largest of the many forest trees.

[3]These figures varied irregularly. Thus later in 1966 when the Buin-Boku road was built through Siwai the rate of compensation was $3 for sago trees and galips, $2.50 for breadfruit trees and $2 for coconuts. (Buin Sub-district Office, Files No. 35-24-2, 35-23-1, 35-32-2. These have since been burnt.)

(b) Sago. The Sago palm *(Metroxylon bougainvillense)* is a remarkable plant with a variety of uses. It flowers only once in its life, at the age of about fifteen years, and just before it is due to flower there is a build-up of starch reserves in the trunk. Boring into the trunk around this time enables the testing of the starch content since, after flowering, it is too late for sago production. The variation in starch content of the sago palm at different periods of its growth is a subject about which very little is known (Townsend 1969). Cutting at the 'wrong' time certainly reduced production and it is unlikely that the 'right'time is always successfully chosen. I suspect that in Siwai the time chosen is later than the optimum since palms are chosen by visual inspection rather than by boring. As elsewhere in Melanesia sago is not simply a food crop; sago leaves form the thatch of roofs and leaf ribs make arrows. Sleeping mats are also made from the leaves and occasionally the bark is used instead of limbum for flooring. The bases of the branches make troughs and finally the rotten stumps provide edible sago grubs. Before the arrival of calico, sago leaves were made into women's skirts and until some time after the war salt was manufactured by burning the base of branches. (The nipa palm *(Nipa fruticans)* was also sometimes used for salt.) The first Siwai 'cash crop' was the fruit of the sago palm; they were traded intermittently until the war. In 1930 Kajewski observed that 'great quantities of the sago palm are collected very year and sold to Japan as ivory nuts of commerce, being used as a substitute for ivory in cheap articles and in the manufacture of buttons' (Kajewski 1946:300); now ivory nuts no longer have a market but make good children's toys.

Sago *(S-bai)* was one of the food trees that Tantanu brought to Siwai but, although it was one of the first cultivated crops, it was Panana (Orphan) who showed them how it should be processed correctly (Oliver 1955: 42-3). Since these mythical times the method of sago production has scarcely changed; Guppy records that a century ago the normal procedure in the Bougainville straits was as follows:

> After the palm has been felled and all the pith removed, either by scooping it out or splitting the trunk, the pith is then torn up into small pieces and placed in a trough extemporised from the broad sheathing base of one of the branches of the felled tree. The trough is then tilted up and is kept filled with water, which running away at the lower end passes through a kind of strainer, made of a fold of the vegetable matting that invests the bases of the branches of the coconut tree, and is then received in another trough of similar material. The fibrous portion of the pith is thus left behind and the sago is deposited as a sediment in the lower trough. When this trough is full of sago, the superfluous water is poured off, and the whole is placed over a fire so as to get rid of the remaining moisture ... The sago is now fit for consumption and is wrapped up in the leaves in the form of cylindrical packages 1½ to 2 feet in length. For the convenience of the water supply, sago-washing is carried out usually on the side of a stream (Guppy 1887:83).[4]

---

[4] A similar account of the process in the Shortland Islands is given by Ribbe (1903:34-6) who also provides an illustration of the bamboo tipped sago adze that was then in use. The basic operations involved in sago production scarcely vary regionally and have been described from a variety of lowland Melanesian settings, such as the Sanio-Hiowe of the Sepik river (Townsend 1969, 1974), Rossel Island, Milne Bay (Armstrong 1928) and the Gadio Enga

He also observed that although most sago was eaten soon after production some could be stored, although this was relatively unusual; although Bougainvilleans had adequate alternative food supplies Guppy thought that they had 'not the forethought of the inhabitants of the Malay Archipelago in laying by a store of sago for future use. When a sago palm is felled, there is usually no lack of friends to assist the owner in consuming the sago' (ibid.:87). Siwais certainly planted sago before the war, whilst Oliver noted that they erected fences round new plants to ensure that they were not crushed by pigs (1955:29). Although there have been no recent sago plantings in Siwai there was considerable planting after the war following destruction of sago palms, primarily because of warfare but also because of depletion by the hungry Japanese army. Sago was planted at least until 1962, since in June of that year the Siwai Local Government Council was discussing on whose ground sago palms could legitimately be planted. Thus sago is to a large extent a cultivated plant, rather than a wild species, in south Bougainville. Currently, supply satisfactorily meets demand and supplies are maintained by the self-germination of seeds.

Production of sago is invariably a team effort; although one man could quite easily carry out the whole process, this neither happened in the past nor does it happen now. Before the war sago production was frequently carried out by a pair of brothers or by a father and his sons, and less frequently by sago teams, made up of men who join together at intervals to help one another prepare sago flour from individually owned palms (Oliver 1955:311); now there are no real sago teams, simply groups with very varied compositions who are unlikely to combine again. Before the war there were regular process lines, divisions of labour where certain men become specialist choppers, shredders, washers and packers; Oliver records that such a team could fell and completely process a sago palm in a single forenoon (1955:311, 434). This team consisted of thirteen adults and the palm was of 'average' size (Oliver, pers. comm. 1976); hence groups were then rather larger than they are now, when it could not be done at this rate. Now too most men are specialists, although work groups are rarely large enough to enable a man to work only at his own speciality. There have also been some minor technological changes; the bamboo-edged adze *(S-kauane)* has been replaced by an adze with a circular metal cutting edge and the coconut matting strainers have been replaced by rice sacks. (In 1975 a group of Siwais had collected $200 to purchase a sago machine to enable commercial production of sago but they had not managed to acquire the machine when I left.)

Production in the prewar era was primarily for domestic consumption and only a small amount of total production was consumed at feasts; exchange and sale of sago was rare. 'An owner will occasionally sell some to a neighbour who is temporarily without taro and sweet potatoes, but most of it is kept in the household as a reserve or as provision for travelling' (Oliver 1955:346-7) when it can easily be carried and roasted.

> During periods of mourning, when the Siwai forego gardening, or during times of continuous rainfall, when they do not like to go to their garden because of the danger of crossing swollen creeks

4 (continued)
of the Central Range of the New Guinea Highlands (Dornstreich 1973). They are also little different in several southeast Asian settings (Ellen 1975:148).

Plate 4. Sago pith being cut frm a felled sago palm, Siroi

Plate 5. Sago processing, Siroi. Sago pith is being squeezed into setting troughs.

Plate 6. Roofing thatch being constructed from sago palm leaves, Turugum

> or the difficulty of walking along slippery paths or the cold discomfort of working in wet and mud, they reluctantly fall back upon sago for their staple' (ibid.:29-30).

Oliver undervalues the satisfaction that most people derived from occasionally eating sago; during periods of heavy rainfall and mourning eating might have been less enjoyable but it seems improbable that a food that was eaten reluctantly would have always been incorporated into feasts, for which sago palm use sometimes had to be rented.

Sago was especially important at times of food shortage such as in the war. During the irregular floods that occur in south Bougainville, sago production has always substantially increased even in the most recent years. In Buin the rains of 1972 (when there were nearly 50 inches in 32 days) caused the resumption of sago production 'which normally is used only at feast periods'. Sago was then one of the six major items in Buin town market (Arndt 1972). In 1957 the patrol officer *(kiap)* Giddings noted that sago was 'usual food' in Siwai but that production had increased because of the heavy rains (Giddings 1958). Indeed sago is ideal as a 'famine food' since it can be produced quickly and can be stored. Nevertheless it is eaten and enjoyed throughout the year at feasts, ordinary meals and brief snacks. Since the starch extracted from the sago palm is almost pure, so that sago is as poor a staple food as any in the world, it is usually supplemented by other foods.

Kiaps, patrolling in south Bougainville after the war, although more interested in the emergence of cash crops, usually observed that sago was a fairly regular part of the diet. In upland Buin, an area ecologically similar to Rataiku, one *kiap*, who mah not have been the most reliable observer, commented that sago shared with sweet potato 'equal main importance in the diet' (Gow 1956). When trees had to be destroyed to make way for new developments, such as roads and airstrips, there was always substantial compensation for sago palms; in 1958 when Konga DASF station was built they were valued at 10s each, the same as coconuts and breadfruit, and in November 1966, when Tonu mission purchased more land, sago palms were valued at \$3, compared with \$2 for coconuts and \$1 for galips. Sago palms were arguably still the most important tree crop in Siwai since mature cocoa trees were then only valued at \$1 each.

Sago production seems to be more common in the south of Siwai, where palms too are more common and access is simple. Not all palms are individually owned; most lineages own unused low-lying ground with 'spare' palms generally available so that there are usually enough for the needs of any one family, even at feast times. Each family in prewar northeast Siwai had an average of 15 sago palms (Oliver 1955:480). This would enable a family to cut at most one tree every year, which is about the present rate of use. I never recorded any purchase of a sago palm for sago production which reflected more their ubiquity than any decline in use. Oliver (1955:434) noted that Soni, who was the most regular giver of large feasts, 'bought' sago palms for these occasions. Like almond trees their inheritance was never in dispute and although access to palms was free, permission for their use for sago production sometimes had to be obtained from the owner. Invariably a group of men from a single lineage would cut a palm belonging to a man from that lineage who would usually himself be engaged in the production.

Apparently unique to south Bougainville is the unusual division of labour; from cutting down the palm to cooking the starch it is entirely men's work whereas in almost all the rest of Melanesia sago production is women's work. (Apart from the minor task of carrying pith from the tree to the stream it is all hard work so that boys younger than teenagers take no part in sago production.) After identification of a suitable palm, ideally as close to a stream as possible, it is felled and a section of the bark removed to expose the fibrous white pith. The section exposed is sufficient for a single day's work; an entire tree demands several days' work, and invariably the whole tree is used up. The sago pith is broken up by repeated pounding with the adze, an extremely arduous activity, normally carried out by a group of men beating in unison. The pith is carried to a trough over the stream where water is added and it is kneaded and squeezed by hand through the sacking strainer, more hard work, into settling troughs. After a few hours the starch can be removed and placed on a drying frame over a fire. This kind of drying enables it to be stored for several months.

Decisions on sago production are usually made by sago palm owners who then organize a work group to produce the sago; such a group is rewarded simply by a proportion of the final product (and irregular meals of sago during the production period). The group is likely to consist of fellow-villagers, men and youths, with no immediate claims on their time, rather than members of a particular lineage. The following example, from Siroi village, seems typical of Siwai sago production organization.

> At the start of December 1974, Ham, a middle-aged man and potential big-man, decided to produce sago from one of the palms on his mother's Lomokera lineage land just to the north of the Siroi line. Since he had cut and dried cocoa from his large plantation the week before he had no particular pressures on his time. On a Monday, during the village work, he collected workers and the palm was cut down the following day, platforms, and troughs were constructed and four men began to cut out the sago pith whilst three more carried the pith to the stream, a hundred feet away, and squeezed it into the drying troughs. This process continued for seven or eight hours a day until the Saturday, although only three of the original workers worked on each of the five days; sometimes there were fewer than seven and sometimes others joined in on odd days. By Saturday afternoon 21 cylinders of sago had been produced from about 25 feet of palm. On Sunday all these were roasted over an open fire. There were then six more feet of palm remaining and on Monday two men sat down to begin crushing the pith from that. One of these was Ham; the other was Kamuai, a man with only a dozen cocoa trees and no nearby land. Ham's sister's son, Uamo, was squeezing the pith. The two men crushed pith from another two feet of tree in the day. On the next day only Ham and, sporadically, Uamo were working; on the Wednesday they completed the work by roasting three more cylinders. From a total expenditure of time of around 40 man-days (of about seven hours each) 24 cylinders of sago weighing about 290 lb were produced. Ham kept four of these (although a week later he gave two of these to a feast-giver at Silaruho); Kamuai, and one other man, received two each and ten other men (two of whom were from Amio) received one each. Ham's father, who was an old man and unable to work, received two (one of which also went to Silaruho), and the other four were divided between seven village households, four of whom were widows, who had not taken part in the

production. Kamuai gave part of his sago to a neighbour so that, in the end, every family in the village received some sago. Most was eaten during the following fortnight, about a tenth was cooked with galip almonds and sold at Monoitu market (especially by the widows) and about a fifth was stored, to be consumed later on.

In the following fifteen months sago production on a similar scale was carried out four more times in Siroi; on only one occasion was production specifically for a feast although even then the composition of the work group was still not organized by lineage affiliation. However, on this occasion villagers who had decided to cut cocoa rather than produce sago were condemned by the sago-workers for their lack of co-operation in a village activity, although none of the absentees was from the feast giver's lineage. The absentees agreed that they should have participated but claimed that their cocoa was over-ripe.

The amount of sago produced by Ham's work group was slightly below average for a single sago palm and since most workers had contributed labour only sporadically, their reward of one cylinder was quite small. Because the size of the cylinder is more or less determined by the size of the sago leaf in which it is wrapped, the quantity of sago in a cylinder is almost uniformly 12 lb. A year later one continuous group produced thirty-one cylinders and nine participants received three cylinders each. On the occasion that sago was produced for a feast six cylinders went to the feast-giver and sixteen were divided up between the workers. In every case production was primarily a village-based activity with distribution of the sago usually eventually reaching every household.

For more or less immediate consumption most sago is wrapped in leaves and roasted above an open fire, although some is mixed with shredded coconut and placed directly in the fire. Often the roasted sago is stored and subsequently made into puddings for eating or selling. European observers tend to agree with Malinowski that, 'the sago produced and eaten by the natives is a tough, starchy stuff of dirty white colour, very unpalatable. It has the consistency of rubber and the taste of very poor, unleavened bread' (Malinowski 1922:378). However, many Siwais, and myself, found sago, especially when mixed into a pudding with galip almonds, a pleasant variation in the diet.

When Siwai sago production is compared with that of specialist sago producers the productivity of Siwai work is very low. In Siwai little more than one pound per man-hour is produced; this compares very unfavourably with Hiowe production of 4.1 pounds per hour and Abelam yields of five pounds per hour, both by female producers in the Sepik district, yields of 8.9 and 10.6 pounds per hour in the lower Sepik region, when men carry out some of the activities (Townsend 1969:38-40) and 6.8 pounds per hour for mainly male producers in the southern Sepik fringes (Dornstreich 1973:211). However, when Siwai production is compared with that of other non-specialist sago producers, such as those of Normanby Island, productivity was much the same as that of the islanders who produced no more than about one and a half pounds in an hour (Schlesier 1965:6-13). Even so Siwai productivity is very low; the main explanation for this is almost certainly the low productivity of Siwai sago palms. There are two main groups of sago palms in Melanesia: a western group, which covers the Sepik and extends as far as New Britain, and an eastern group which includes Bougainvillean sago (Crosby 1976:138). Unfortunately there are no other measures of the productivity of this eastern group; indeed south Bougainville now seems to be the present easternmost centre of sago production, a remnant of a sago-eating area that may once have extended as far east as Fiji and was present in Tikopia and Malaita at least until after the last war. Even in Bougainvillean terms it is possible that Siwai sago may be relatively unproductive; thus Sumbak states that 'sago palm development is also reported to be poor in the Buin (sub-district) area' (1970:4). In the village of Busama in the Morobe district of New Guinea, which seems to be the easternmost area where sago production has been observed carefully, Hogbin recorded that villagers produced only about 400 to 500 pounds of sago from a single palm where Sepiks might produce 700 pounds; yet this was a reference to working methods rather than to the palms themselves. His servant who came from Sepik stated that 'his mother would have wept with annoyance at the sight of such inefficiency' (Hogbin 1951:72). It may be that Siwais are similarly wasteful converters of pith into sago. Siwai times include all time spent on site, hence about two-thirds of this represents the actual hard work of producing sago. Moreover more of this work is wasted since each cubic foot of pith produces only three pounds of sago, compared with 6.25 pounds in Hiowe and 14.7 pounds in Abelam (Townsend 1969:38-40), although since some pith is consumed by Siwai pigs there is less 'wastage' than these figures imply. (My data are insufficient to be conclusive but they do not suggest that large sago work groups are more productive than one or two men.) Production of sago in Siwai may be hard work but it is not unproductive in terms of energy expended; comparing the number of man-hours required to produce a million calories it seems that Siwai production (in which 430 man-hours are required)[5] is equivalent to the more intensive agricultural systems. The greatest value of the sago palm is that it is always available for sago production and that it has a variety of alternative uses; moreover ease of production makes a storable economic surplus always possible.

On each occasion that sago palms were cut for sago production the leaves remained unused except for wrapping the sago; palms for thatch were always cut separately and I never recorded any sago palm leaves being sold for domestic uses. Before the war palm leaves were 'not infrequently made up into roof-thatching sheets for sale ... if a man wishes to build a club-house ... no individual owns enough sago palms or controls enough labour to manufacture so many sheets within the allotted time ... Five sheets sell for only one *mauai*' (Oliver 1955:347). On one occasion in 1975 during the construction of a men's club house *(S-kaposo)* at Turugum the owner rewarded villagers from Mokolino and Maisua who brought thatch ready made from their own trees. The owner had enough trees of his own; the thatchmakers merely preferred to work at home. Now, especially in central Siwai, there is never a shortage of palms, even during *kaposo* construction; some are destroyed profligately and leaves are never purchased.

Elsewhere in Bougainville, although sago plays some part in social and economic life, its food role has been generally ignored in ethnographic studies of other areas and mention is only made of the use of the leaves as thatch. In Buin Laycock (1975:211) observed that sago was an important staple at large feasts but played little part in daily life. Mitchell (1976) surprisingly makes no mention of sago processing in neighbouring Nagovisi, although the organization of the economy seems to be otherwise little different from Siwai, whilst Ogan (1972) does not mention any

---

[5]This analysis followed that of Townsend (1969, 1974).

contemporary use amongst the Nasioi. Rutherford (1974:58) stated that the Aita of upland Bougainville knew how to prepare sago but that it was not done because it required a huge amount of labour for a comparatively small return of food. (It is not clear if this is the perception of Rutherford or of the Aita.) On the north Bougainville coast the people did not normally eat sago except in times of scarcity (Blackwood 1935:288). On parts of the east coast the organization of production is quite different; women play a much more important role in processing and in upland Kongara at least the pith is squeezed by trampling on a platform. Its contribution to the subsistence economy is however greatest on the wet western coast and probably very significant in more isolated parts of Banoni and Keriaka. In Siwai it remains of considerable value.

(c) Other trees and shrubs. Wild trees and other plants provide a range of products of use for food, medicine, handicrafts and construction; since data were not collected systematically on several of these topics this brief account inevitably undervalues the role of these plants.[6]

The most regular use of trees is for the collection of firewood (almost always by women), which, unusually, has domestic, commercial and ritual uses. Firewood must be collected during the first of the growth magic rituals but on this occasion it merely substitutes for domestic collection; at other times large quantities may be consumed during the preparation of feasts. Ordinarily firewood is used for domestic cooking and most households maintain a fire day and night; although a handful of Siwai families have purchased kereosene cookers none use them regularly. Demands for domestic firewood are therefore considerable and are sometimes met by inter-household exchange. Increasingly the greatest demand is from copra and cocoa driers which consume considerable quantities of firewood and must be maintained for two or three days at a time. Although owners of small driers so far seem to have met demands from their own land, without even cutting wood specially, the Siwai Society is not so fortunate. It must buy all its firewood requirements and purchases two or three truckloads a week. In 1975 two Siroi villagers, neither of whom had much cocoa, were selling regularly to the Society. Each sold two trailer loads and each received $12. Although some Siwais are becoming concerned about the depletion of bush and therefore firewood, the range of trees that are useable is enormous hence, although collection is confined to within the land of one's lineage, anyone is at present able to meet all his requirements from his own garden clearing.

Ironwood (S-moikui; Vitex monophylla) is the most important wood for construction activity, forming the basic posts and girders of ordinary houses and also the men's club house *(S-kaposo)*. It is also the wood from which the slit gongs *(S-tui)* placed inside the house are carved from. Ironwood is an exceptionally hard and heavy wood and would be wasted as firewood for which it would be badly suited. The other wood used in house construction is the black palm or limbum *(Kentsiopsis spp.)* which is also a very hard wood, with the additional advantage that it is almost impossible to burn, hence it is useful as flooring and as supporting lathes in roofs. Limbum

---

[6]Data on flora refer mainly to casual observations in central Siwai. It is probable that there were substantial variations in the north and south (especially on the coast) in the range and quantity of utilized forest products.

is also used for bows. Either plaited sago leaves or several kinds of bamboo *(Bambusa* spp.) are used for house walls. Bamboo is also used for making combs and lime containers, which in small quantities are now primarily an exported tourist commodity, and panpipes. Bamboos are also used to store smoked almonds but unlike in more mountainous parts of Bougainville are not used for either carrying water or cooking. Some Siwais occasionally manufacture cane furniture from rattan palms *(Calamus* spp.) but the general decline in handicraft production meant that none were being made in 1975. Record (1945) lists some thirty-two trees at least which had some economic importance in Siwai for construction and related activities. Some of these uses have now completely disappeared, such as ceremonial hat manufacture using *ohkuna (Licuala lauterbachii)* and the use of a special kind of wood *(S-inuku; Perrotteria grandiflora)* for making fire by friction. Most remain important. None of these trees are ever planted and none are individually owned; access to ironwood and limbum would normally be limited to lineage ground.

Ropes and vines are used in some phases of house construction but are much more important in the construction of men's club houses, where nails are not traditionally used (although, now, vines are occasionally reinforced by nails at strategic points). The main source of this kind of binding is the rattan palm. Siwai baskets and fish traps are made from the split stems of the large vines *(S-koruwoi; Lygodium* spp.) which is bound into a framework consisting of the whole stem of another fern species. The vines themselves are often sold in Siwai markets. The vines collected for basket-weaving are considered by some Siwais to be declining in quantity (and therefore accessibility), a decline which parallels a move from basket-weaving to cocoa-growing, and a consequent lack of interest in finding the vines. This was the only reference made to the decline of any useful plant species and, in this case, may be untrue. Temporary baskets for food distribution and more permanent baskets for carrying garden produce are made from coconut leaves; small ornamental shoulder baskets and flat folding 'umbrellas' are made from pandanus leaves and sago leaves respectively. Both 'umbrellas' and string bags are now rarely made. Similarly there are now no locally manufactured cooking implements; everything comes from stores. Digging sticks and axe handles are still locally produced; although purchased axes now satisfy all Siwais, several men make a small income from making and selling new handles.

A wide range of leaves from wild trees and shrubs are used for both green vegetables and medicines; most of these I never identified and the remainder I knew only by their Si-ai names. A range of edible fungi *(S-kutowa; Auricolia* spp.) existed and were regularly collected, especially from newly cleared sites. The most popular source of leafy vegetables available from the bush was the 'tulip' tree *(Gnetum gnemon, S-marewa)* whose bark can also be used for making twine. Other identifiable species include taro and sweet potato leaves and vine leaves *(Ipomoea aquatica)*. One random Siwai alone listed twelve more kinds of wild vegetables (picked rather than dug) which were not identified, whilst Pitt recorded in 1960 that 'the Siwai people eat thirty different kinds of leaves to provide a leafy vegetable in their diet. None or very few of these leaves are cultivated but are collected from the bush' (Pitt 1960). In addition a range of ferns is eaten, particularly with pork at feasts. There remain other plants, especially wild tubers, such as the various species of wild yams *(S-kormuoka, ituku; Dioscorea* spp.) and bananas that are rarely eaten now but could easily be collected and eaten again in times of need. Wild yams were eaten during the war. This by no means exhausts the list of wild species that can be collected and used at various times; a wide range of plants, especially croton and ginger, are used for medicinal purposes (and magic). A fairly complete description of the edible plant species of Siwai could be compiled by distinguishing the useful plants from Foreman's (1971) compilation of the historic collections of Waterhouse, Kajewski and the Rechingers. This would not, however, completely verify that these species existed and were used in Siwai after the war; nor would it prove their present use and distribution.

Gathering has always been primarily a women's activity. Before the war, as now, a woman going to her gardens will be constantly on the lookout for green vegetables and other wild plant foods. 'In such matters women are the experts, knowing where wild plants are to be found, and how they should be collected and prepared. Sometimes a woman may be fortunate enough to find edible mushrooms, funguses and flower buds, or snails, grubs and white ants' (Oliver 1955:136). Women still provide the bulk of gathered vegetables but it is not unusual to see men collecting them, especially whilst looking for basket vines, and children often collect greens. Collected foods represent only a small proportion of the diet (although a large part of the green vegetable component) but they tend to be regularly and easily obtained, abundant and available to anyone who wants them.

The forage economy

Recent accounts of other Bougainvillean (and lowland Melanesian) societies have largely ignored hunting and gathering; Mitchell (1976) does not mention hunting and gathering in the context of neighbouring Nagovisi but in Buin, where historical practice was apparently identical with Siwai, contemporary pig hunting still seems to be the same, in organization and returns, as Siwai (Laycock 1975:205). It seems probable that in most of west coast Bougainville practices are broadly similar to those of Siwai but on the east coast the availability of game, either in rivers or on the land, is substantially depleted but compensated by the availability of salt-water fish. Despite the introduction of the gun, much of Siwai hunting, gathering and fishing activity continues almost unchanged; the contribution of each to the diet, and even to ceremonials, may be small but it is not falling. The range and quantity of foods remain almost unchanged. Cocoa growing has absorbed more labour, hence less time is now spent on hunting, although this decline is balanced by the arrival of the shotgun. Nevertheless, unlike most parts of Bougainville, there is continuity without substantial change.

Siwai hunting and gathering has almost nothing in common with those societies largely without gardens and dependent upon a forage economy for the major part of their diet. If all wild species disappeared from Siwai overnight there would be no resulting problems; the basic food supply would continue to be gardens supplemented by purchases from trade stores. Limited effort put into hunting reflect a lack of concern with success in food procurement; moreover there is little prestige, but considerable satisfaction, derived from even the most successful hunting trip. Hunting is generally a pleasurable activity but with considerable social and economic benefits; consequently Oliver's summary of Siwai hunting and gathering as 'ineffective' (1961:57) is, in my experience, inaccurate and also undervalues the enjoyment drived from hunting. The lack of seasons in Siwai is reflected in hunting and gathering activity. Only the sea turtle and a few plants such as galip almonds have seasons although moonlight nights encourage a monthly cycle in hunting activity. Most species can be hunted and gathered throughout the year; the time spent is small and does not hinder ordinary gardening activities. Hunting is now solely for meat; possum fur is not valued as decoration and the bones of flying foxes are no longer used as needles.

Pig hunting especially remains a skilled activity; knowledge of the wild pigs' habits and knowledge of trap setting are dying, but so too are the wild pigs. In the past it is probable that these were not specialist skills; all adult males had access to this knowledge and possibly even to the attendant hunting magic (which has now disappeared in entirety). There are few skills that need to be communicated; hunting and fishing are simple affairs that most people enjoy. Nevertheless hunting is usually a young man's activity and gathering is less enjoyable women's work. Hunting for pigs, possums, flying foxes and birds and also sago making are the only exclusive male activities, outside of ceremonials. In most circumstances hunting is a pleasure and the bag almost an extra bonus; usually no one hunts who does not enjoy it and it is a good way of breaking up the monotony of life. But there are differences from a European situation; it is extremely difficult to purchase most kinds of game, hence the desire that many Siwais express at some time for 'fresh meat' can only be met by hunting. Hunting is therefore more frequent and provides a greater part of the protein component in the diet although its absolute contribution is small. Ceremonials place a special demand on hunting and on a few occasions parties may consist of some unwilling hunters; ritual demands boost hunting activity. There are no real demands on gatherers, although large quantities of ferns are required at feasts since pigs are always cooked and eaten with them.

Unlike other areas of Melanesia, such as amongst the Rofaifo of the New Guinea Highlands (Dwyer 1974) where game must be distributed to a wide category of relatives, a Siwai hunter has no need to distribute a kill beyond his immediate family on hunts other than those specifically for ceremonials.

The existence of large extents of 'bush', developed from secondary gardens often over periods longer than twenty years, even in the most densely populated central areas of Siwai, ensures that a wide range of products of various kinds can be freely gathered there. Moreover the existence of this bush, and more particularly the natural tropical forest of the coastal belt and the mountains, provides a home for various kinds of hunted game, which also share in much of the forage available. Indeed the superior flavour of wild pig,as in Santa Cruz (Yen 1974:276) is sometimes attributed to its varied bush diet. On the other hand as Bulmer (1968) has observed elsewhere, some of these creatures, especially wild pigs and sago grubs, have been encouraged to live in their present environments in Siwai by man's agricultural activities. Despite concern over the depletion of the forests and some of its wildlife, especially possums (which are necessary for some rituals), hunting and foraging remain a significant part of subsistence activity, and that situation is unlikely to change in the near future. The forage economy provides a significant quantity of food both for domestic meals and for feasts, and, even more important, immensely broadens the range of available food mainly by providing a majority of the most prized foods in Siwai diets. Hunting and gathering scarcely compete for time or labour with other subsistence activities or even cocoa growing; for a small input of time this land-rich area provides a considerable bonus of varied foods, and other goods, most of which can also be marketed. Moreover, again with limited exceptions, access to these resources is free and only a fraction of edible species are used. The forage economy is a selective and specialized, but not intensive, exploitation of the forest. Human activities have only marginally altered the distribution of sought-after species. Hunting and gathering make a greater contribution to the Siwai economy than has been recorded for other contemporary Bougainvillean societies which are usually regarded simply as swidden agriculturalists. Siwais continue to be both hunter-gatherers and horticulturalists.

Bibliography

Anon., 1934. 'Scientists in New Guinea', *Pacific Islands Monthly*, 5 June.

Armstrong, W.E., 1928. *Rossel Island: An Ethnological Study*, Cambridge.

Arndt, F., 1972. ' Investigations on reports of food shortages due to garden damage caused by excessive rains in the Buin sub-district', DASF, Kieta, mimeo.

Blackwood, B., 1931. 'Mountain people of the South Seas', *Natural History*, 31:424-33.

-- 1935. *Both Sides of Buka Passage*, Oxford.

Bulmer, R.N.H., 1968. 'The strategies of hunting in New Guinea', *Oceania*, 38 (4):302-18.

Crosby, E., 1976. 'Sago in Melanesia', *Archaeology and Physical Anthropology in Oceania*, 11 (2), July:138-55.

Dornstreich, M.D., 1973. 'An ecological study of Gadio Enga (New Guinea) subsistence', Ph.D. thesis, Columbia University.

Dwyer, P.D., 1974. 'The price of protein: five hundred hours of hunting in the New Guinea Highlands', *Oceania*, 44 (4), June:278-93.

Ellen, R.F., 1972. 'The marsupial in Nuaulu ritual behaviour', *Man*, 7 (2): 223-38.

-- 1975. 'Non-domesticated resources in Nuaulu ecological relations', *Social Science Information*, 14 (5):127-50.

Foreman, D.B., 1971. *A Check List of the Vascular Plants of Bougainville with Descriptions of Some Common Forest Trees*, Botany Bulletin No.5, Department of Forests, Division of Botany, Lae.

Franke, C.S., 1950. Annual Report of the Agricultural Extension Service, Buin Sub-district, July 1949-June 1950, mimeo, 8 pp. (PNG National Archives, Port Moresby, Box 4241. File 38-2-10.)

French, B.R., 1969. Letter to ADC, Buin, 20 November (DASF Konga File 14-4d).

Giddings, R.J., 1958. Siwai. Patrol Report Boku No.1/1957-58.

Gow, A.F., 1956. Lugakei. Patrol Report Buin No.2/1955-56.

Guppy, H.B., 1887. *The Solomon Islands and their Natives*, London.

Hogbin, H.I., 1951. *Transformation Scene. The Changing Culture of a New Guinea Village*, London.

Hook, D.J., 1956. Siwai. Patrol Report Boku No.3/1955-56.

-- 1957. Banoni. Patrol Report Boku No.2/1956-57.

Kajewski, S.F., 1946. 'Plant collecting in the Solomon Islands', *Journal of the Arnold Arboretum*, 27 (3):292-304.

Laycock, D., 1975. 'Butchering pigs in Buin', *Journal of the Polynesian Society*, 84 (2), June:203-12.

Malinowski, B., 1922. *Argonauts of the Western Pacific*, London.

McCabe, B.A., 1956. Nasioi. Patrol Report Kieta No.2/1955-56.

Mitchell, D.D., 1977. *Gardening for Money*, in press, Port Moresby.

Ogan, E., 1972. 'Business and cargo: socio-economic change among the Nasioi of Bougainville', *New Guinea Research Bulletin* No.44, Canberra.

Oliver, D.L., 1949. 'Studies in the anthropology of Bougainville, Solomon Islands', *Papers of the Peabody Museum*, 29 (four parts).

-- 1955. *A Solomon Island Society. Kinship and Leadership among the* Siuai *of Bougainville*, Harvard.

-- 1961. *The Pacific Islands*, New York (2nd ed.).

Parkinson, R.F., 1907. *Thirty Years in the South Seas*, Stuttgart (English trans. N.C. Barry).

Pitt, A.D., 1960. Siwai. Patrol Report Boku No.2/1960-61.

Reading, J.M., 1965. Banoni. Patrol Report Boku No.4/1964-65.

Record, M., 1945. 'A collection of woody plants from Melanesia', *Tropical Woods*, 81 (1), March:9-45.

Ribbe, C., 1903. *Zwei Jahre unter den Cannibalen der Salomo-Inseln*, Dresden.

Ross, H.M., 1973. 'Baegu. Social and ecological organization in Malaita, Solomon Islands', *Illinois Studies in Anthropology*, No.8, Urbana.

Rutherford, J., 1974. 'Mobile agriculturalists: land and population exchanges in the social organization of the Bougainville Aita', Honolulu, unpub. ms.

Sarei, A.H., 1974. 'Traditional marriage and the impact of Christianity on the Solos of Buka Island', *New Guinea Research Bulletin*, No.57, Canberra.

Scheffler, H.W., 1965. *Choiseul Island Social Structure*, Berkeley and Los Angeles.

Schlesier, E., 1965. 'Sagogewinnung auf Normanby Island, Sudost Neuguinea', *Baessler-Archiv*, 13:1-39.

Sumbak, J.H., 1970. 'Poor coconut growth in South West Bougainville', *Papua and New Guinea Agricultural Journal*, 22 (1), December:1-5.

Townsend, P.K.W., 1969. Subsistence and social organization in a New Guinea society, Ph.D. thesis, University of Michigan.

Townsend, P.K., 1974. 'Sago production in a New Guinea economy', *Human Ecology*, 2 (3), July:217-36.

Treide, B., 1967. *Wildpflanzen in der Ernährung der Grundbevölkerung Melanesiens*, Berlin.

Voyce, A.H., 1957. 'The Siuai of Bougainville' (review), *International Review of Missions*, 46 (1):106-8.

Yen, D.E., 1974. 'Arboriculture in the subsistence of Santa Cruz, Solomon Islands', *Economic Botany*, 28 (3), July-September:247-84.

DEVELOPMENT STUDIES CENTRE PUBLICATIONS

Monographs

No.1 Labour and the Law in Papua New Guinea, D.W. Smith, 1975. $A4.00.

No.2 The role of the Papua New Guinea Defence Force, Paul Mench, 1976. $A6.00

No.3 Education, employment and migration in Papua New Guinea, J.D. Conroy, 1976. $A6.00

No.4 Chimbu: issues in development, Diana Howlett, R. Hide and Elspeth Young with J. Arba, H. Bi and B. Kaman, 1976. $A6.00

No.5 Professional structure in Southeast Asia, ed. T.H.Silcock, 1977. $A6.00

Occasional papers

No.1 Motivational factors affecting Bougainville villagers' money earning activity, T.K. Moulik, 1975. $A2.00

No.2 Food dependency in the Pacific: a preliminary statement, T.G. McGee, 1975. $A2.00

No.3 Burma's rice surpluses: accounting for the decline, H.V. Richter, 1976. $A2.00

No.4 The fading of earthbound compulsion in a Hong Kong village: population mobility and its economic implication, Rance Pui-leung Lee, 1976. $A2.00

No.5 The defence forces of small states: a comparison of defence statistics in 26 states of Tropical Africa, Papua New Guinea and Fiji, Paul Mench, 1976. $A2.00

No.6 Hunting and gathering: the forage economy of the Siwai of Bougainville, John Connell, 1977. $A2.00

MADE Research Series

No.1 The dynamic replacement problem in the rubber industry of Sri Lanka, S.K.W. Jayasuriya, 1976. $A5.00

No.2 Rational farm plans for land settlement in Indonesia, M.A. Wardhani, 1976. $A5.00

Thesis Abstracts

No.1 Studies in the economics of agricultural development, D.M. Etherington and B. Carrad (eds), 1976. $A3.00

Publications are available from the Development Studies Centre, A. Block, The Australian National University, P.O. Box 4, Canberra, 2600, A.C.T. Please enclose money with order.